MEAT
CLASSICS

Consultant Editor:
Valerie Ferguson

LORENZ BOOKS

Contents

Introduction

Meat plays a leading role in most of the cuisines of the world and has featured in the human diet from prehistoric times to the present day. The most popular meats eaten in the Western world are beef, including veal; pork, gammon, ham and bacon; lamb and poultry. It is an excellent source of protein, containing all eight amino acids essential for the body, as well as many B complex vitamins and minerals, such as iron and zinc. In general, cheaper cuts take longer to cook than expensive ones but are, nevertheless, as nutritious.

Widely available and immensely versatile, meat can be cooked in just about every possible way. It may be served plain or with a sauce, cooked rapidly with other ingredients or slow-cooked with vegetables and herbs so that the flavours mingle. Different cuts are best suited to different cooking techniques, such as roasting, braising, stewing, pan-frying, grilling, stir-frying and barbecuing.

The recipes in this book range from traditional favourites such as Steak, Kidney & Mushroom Pie and Roast Chicken, to more adventurous dishes including Lamb Korma or Thai Pork Satay with Peanut Sauce. *Meat Classics* provides inspiration for every occasion throughout the year.

Techniques

PREPARING MEAT FOR COOKING

You can buy meat ready for cooking from butchers, but some cuts need further preparation, as shown in the techniques below.

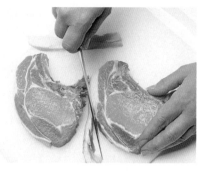

1 To trim: Use a sharp knife to trim skin or rind and fat from the surface. Leave a little fat on steaks to be grilled and slash it at regular intervals to prevent the steak curling up. Roasts should retain a thin layer (about 3–5 mm/⅛–¼ in) of fat. Cut away the sinews and tough connective tissue.

2 To bard a joint: If very lean meat is to be roasted without a protective crust (a spice mixture or pastry, for example), it is a good idea to bard it to keep it moist. Wrap very thin slices of beef fat, pork fat or blanched bacon around the joint and tie them in place.

3 To tie a boned joint: Boned joints should be tied into a neat shape for roasting or pot roasting. The butcher will do this, but if you want to add a stuffing or seasoning, you will need to retie the joint. Reshape it into a neat, even roll. Use butcher's string to make ties around the joint at 2.5 cm/1 in intervals. Noisettes can be prepared from best end of lamb. Ease out the ribs and roll up starting from the meaty end. Tie and cut into 5 cm/ 2 in slices.

HOW MUCH TO BUY
When buying boneless meat that has little or no fat, allow 150– 200 g/5–7 oz per serving. For meat with bone that has a little fat at the edge, allow about 225 g/8 oz per serving. Very bony cuts, such as spare ribs, have proportionally little meat so you will need 450 g/1 lb per serving.

ROASTING MEAT

The dry heat of oven roasting is best suited to tender cuts. If they have no natural marbling of fat, bard them. Alternatively, marinate the meat or baste it frequently with the roasting juices during cooking.

Meat to be roasted should be at room temperature. Roast on a rack in a tin a little larger than the joint. Without a rack, the base of the joint would stew and not become crisp.

There are two methods of roasting meat. For the first, the joint is seared at a high temperature and then the heat is reduced for the remainder of the cooking time. For the second method, the joint is roasted at a constant temperature throughout. Studies have shown that both methods produce good results, and that it is prolonged cooking, not the method, that affects juiciness and causes shrinkage.

1 According to the recipe, rub the joint with oil or butter and season. For extra flavour, make little slits all over the surface with the tip of a sharp knife. Insert flavourings, such as herbs, slivers of garlic or olive slices.

2 Roast the joint for the time suggested in the chart below, basting the meat if necessary.

3 Transfer the cooked meat to a carving board. Leave it to rest for 10–15 minutes before carving.

SUGGESTED ROASTING TIMES

Following the second roasting method, in a 180°C/350°F/Gas 4 oven, approximate timings in minutes per 450 g/1 lb:

Beef, rare, 20 + 20 extra ★
medium, 25 + 25 extra
well done, 30 + 30 extra
Veal, 25 + 25 extra
Lamb, 25 + 25 extra
Pork, 35 + 35 extra
(★ Prime cuts such as a joint of beef and tenderloin need less time.)

Chicken in a 190°C/375°F/
Gas 5 oven
1.2–1.3 kg/2½–3 lb, 1–1¼ hours
1.5–1.75 kg/3½–4 lb, 1¼–1¾ hours
2–2.25 kg/4½–5 lb, 1½–2 hours
2.25–2.75 kg/5–6 lb, 1¾–2½ hours

TESTING TO DETERMINE WHEN MEAT IS COOKED

The cooking times given in a recipe are intended as guidelines. The shape of a cut can affect how long it takes to cook, and people have different preferences for how well cooked they like meat to be. So testing is essential.

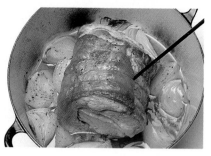

1 Large joints that are roasted or pot-roasted can be tested with a metal skewer. Insert the skewer into the thickest part and leave it in place for 30 seconds. Withdraw the skewer and feel it: if it is warm, the meat is rare; if it is hot, the meat is well cooked.

2 The most reliable test is with a meat thermometer, inserted in the the joint. The manufacturer's instructions will include temperature readings for each type of meat.

NATURAL LAW OF ROASTING
A joint will continue to cook in its own retained heat for 5–10 minutes after being removed from oven or pot, so it is a good idea to take it out when it is just below the desired thermometer reading.

Gravy

Gravy made from the roasting juices is rich in flavour and colour. It is a traditional accompaniment for roast meat and poultry.

1 Spoon off most of the fat from the roasting tin. Set the tin over a moderately high heat. When the roasting juices begin to sizzle, add flour and stir to combine well.

2 Cook, scraping the tin well to mix in all the browned bits from the base, until the mixture forms a smooth brown paste. Add stock and bring to the boil, stirring or whisking constantly. Simmer until reduced, then season with salt and pepper.

Meat Stock

The most delicious meat soups, stews, casseroles, gravies and sauces rely on a good home-made stock for success.

INGREDIENTS
30 ml/2 tbsp vegetable oil
1.5 kg/3–3½ lb shin, shank or
  neck of beef bones,
  cut into pieces
225 g/8 oz shin of beef,
  cut into pieces
bouquet garni
2 onions, quartered
2 carrots, chopped
2 celery sticks, sliced
5 ml/1 tsp whole black
  peppercorns
2.5 ml/½ tsp salt

2 Transfer the meat and bones to a large saucepan, add the remaining ingredients and cover with 3.2 litres 5½ pints/14 cups water. Bring to the boil, skim the surface with a spoon, then partially cover and simmer for 2½–3 hours, or until reduced to 1.6 litres/2¾ pints/6½ cups.

1 Preheat the oven to 220°C/ 425°F/Gas 7. Drizzle the vegetable oil over the bottom of a roasting tin and swirl the tin to cover the base. Add the beef bones and meat. Toss well to coat in the oil and bake for 25–30 minutes, or until well browned, turning regularly during cooking to ensure even browning.

3 Strain the stock into a bowl. Cool and remove the solidified fat before use. The stock can be stored for up to 4 days in the fridge.

Roast Beef with Mushrooms & Roasted Sweet Peppers

A substantial and warming dish for cold, dark evenings, this would make an excellent choice for a dinner party.

Serves 8

INGREDIENTS

1.5 kg/3–3½ lb piece of sirloin
15 ml/1 tbsp olive oil
450 g/1 lb small red peppers
175 g/6 oz thick-sliced pancetta or smoked bacon, diced
50 g/2 oz/2 tbsp plain flour
150 ml/¼ pint/⅔ cup full-bodied red wine
300 ml/½ pint/1¼ cups beef stock
30 ml/2 tbsp Marsala
10 ml/2 tsp dried mixed herbs
115 g/4 oz mushrooms, roughly chopped
salt and freshly ground black pepper

1 Preheat the oven to 190°C/375°F/ Gas 5. Season the meat well all over. Heat the olive oil in a large frying pan and brown the meat on all sides. Place in a large roasting tin and cook for 1¼ hours.

2 Put the red peppers in the oven to roast for 20 minutes, if small ones are available, or 45 minutes if large ones are used.

3 Near the end of the meat's cooking time, prepare the gravy. Heat the frying pan again and add the pancetta or bacon. Cook until the fat runs. Add the flour and cook for a few minutes until browned.

4 Gradually stir in the red wine and the stock. Bring to the boil, stirring. Lower the heat and add the Marsala, herbs and seasoning.

5 Add the mushrooms to the pan and heat through. Remove the sirloin from the oven and leave to stand for 10 minutes before carving it. Serve with the roasted peppers and the hot gravy.

Steak, Kidney & Mushroom Pie

One of Britain's best-known dishes, this satisfying pie is perfect for a family supper on a cold winter's evening.

Serves 4

INGREDIENTS
30 ml/2 tbsp vegetable oil
115 g/4 oz bacon, chopped
1 onion, chopped
500 g/1¼ lb chuck steak, diced
30 ml/2 tbsp plain flour
115 g/4 oz lambs' kidneys
large bouquet garni
400 ml/14 fl oz/1⅔ cups beef stock
115 g/4 oz/1½ cups button mushrooms
225 g/8 oz ready-made
   puff pastry
beaten egg, to glaze
salt and freshly ground
   black pepper

1 Preheat the oven to 160°C/325°F/
Gas 3. Heat the oil in a heavy-based pan and cook the bacon and onion until lightly browned.

2 Toss the steak in the flour. Stir the meat into the pan in batches and cook, stirring, until browned.

3 Toss the kidneys in flour and add to the pan with the bouquet garni. Transfer to a casserole, pour in the stock, cover and cook in the oven for 2 hours. Stir in the mushrooms and seasoning and leave to cool.

4 Preheat the oven to 220°C/425°F/ Gas 7. Roll out the pastry to 2 cm/ ¾ in larger than the top of a 1.2 litre/ 2 pint/5 cup pie dish. Cut off a narrow strip and fit around the dampened rim of the dish. Brush the pastry strip with water.

5 Tip the meat mixture into the dish. Lay the pastry over the dish. Press the edges together to seal decoratively using two fingers on top and one to push the edge inwards. Use a knife to knock up the edges.

6 Top with pastry leaves. Make a small slit in the pastry, brush with beaten egg and bake for 20 minutes. Lower the oven temperature to 180°C/350°F/Gas 4 and bake for a further 20 minutes until the pastry is risen, golden and crisp.

Beef Stew with Red Wine

This rich, hearty Italian dish is satisfying and tasty served with mashed potatoes, rice or polenta and lightly steamed vegetables.

Serves 6

INGREDIENTS
75 ml/5 tbsp olive oil
1.2 kg/2½ lb boneless beef chuck, cut into
    4 cm/1½ in cubes
1 medium onion, very thinly sliced
2 carrots, chopped
45 ml/3 tbsp finely chopped fresh parsley
1 clove garlic, chopped
1 bay leaf
a few sprigs fresh thyme, or pinch of
    dried thyme leaves
pinch of ground nutmeg
250 ml/8 fl oz/1 cup red wine
400 g/14 oz can plum tomatoes, chopped,
    with their juice
120 ml/4 fl oz/½ cup beef or
    chicken stock
about 15 black olives, stoned
    and halved
1 large red pepper, cut into strips
salt and freshly ground black pepper

1 Preheat the oven to 180°C/350°F/
Gas 4. Heat 45 ml/3 tbsp of the oil
in a large, heavy casserole. Brown the
meat, a little at a time, turning it to
colour on all sides.

2 Remove the meat and add the
remaining oil, the onion and
carrots. Cook over a low heat until the
onion softens. Add the parsley and
garlic, and cook for 3–4 minutes.

3 Return the meat to the pan, raise
the heat, and stir well to mix. Stir
in the bay leaf, thyme and nutmeg.
Add the wine, bring to the boil and
cook, stirring, for 4–5 minutes. Stir in
the tomatoes, stock and olives, and mix
well. Season, cover and bake in the
oven for 1½ hours.

4 Remove the casserole from the
oven. Stir in the strips of pepper.
Return the casserole to the oven and
cook, uncovered, for 30 minutes more,
or until the beef is tender.

Steak au Poivre

There are many versions of this French bistro classic. Some omit the cream, but it helps to balance the heat of the pepper.

Serves 2

INGREDIENTS
30 ml/2 tbsp black peppercorns
2 fillet or sirloin steaks, about 225 g/
    8 oz each
15 g/½ oz/1 tbsp butter
10 ml/2 tsp vegetable oil
45 ml/3 tbsp brandy
150 ml/¼ pint/⅔ cup
    whipping cream
1 garlic clove, finely chopped
salt (optional)

1 Place the peppercorns in a sturdy plastic bag and crush with a rolling pin until medium-coarse. Alternatively, use a pestle and mortar.

2 Put the steaks on a board and trim away any extra fat. Press the pepper on to both sides of the meat, coating it completely. Melt the butter with the oil in a heavy frying pan over a medium-high heat.

3 Add the meat and cook it for 6–7 minutes, turning once, until done as preferred. Transfer the steaks to serving plates and keep warm.

4 Pour in the brandy to deglaze the pan. Allow to boil until reduced by half, scraping the base of the pan, then add the cream and garlic. Boil the sauce gently over a medium heat for about 4 minutes until it has reduced by one-third. Stir any accumulated juices from the meat into the sauce, taste and add salt, if necessary, then serve the steaks with the sauce.

Hungarian Beef Goulash

A good goulash is made rich and smooth with onions and paprika. In this recipe, dark field mushrooms and morel mushrooms provide extra flavour.

Serves 4

INGREDIENTS
900 g/2 lb chuck steak, diced
60 ml/4 tbsp vegetable oil
150 ml/¼ pint/⅔ cup red wine
4 medium onions, halved and sliced
450 g/1 lb/6 cups field or horse mushrooms
    or closed shaggy ink caps, trimmed
    and chopped
45 ml/3 tbsp mild paprika
600 ml/1 pint/2½ cups beef stock
30 ml/2 tbsp tomato purée
15 g/½ oz/¼ cup dried morel mushrooms,
    soaked in warm water for
    20 minutes
15 ml/1 tbsp wine vinegar
salt and freshly ground black pepper
jacket potatoes, Savoy cabbage and carrots,
    to serve

1 Preheat the oven to 160°C/325°F/ Gas 3 and season the meat with pepper. Heat half the vegetable oil in a large heavy-based frying pan and fry the meat over a high heat, turning once, until browned.

2 Transfer to a flameproof casserole and pour off the fat. Return the frying pan to the heat, add the wine and stir with a flat wooden spoon to deglaze. Pour the liquid over the meat and wipe the pan clean with kitchen paper.

3 Heat the remaining oil in the pan, add the onions and sauté for 5–7 minutes, stirring frequently, until lightly browned and soft.

4 Add the fresh mushrooms, paprika, stock, tomato purée, the morels and their liquid to the casserole. Bring to a simmer, cover and cook in the oven for about 1½ hours until the meat is meltingly tender.

5 Just before serving, add the vinegar and adjust the seasoning, if necessary. Serve with jacket potatoes, Savoy cabbage and carrots.

COOK'S TIP: Goulash can also be made with diced pork or veal. In this case use chicken stock in place of beef. To keep the goulash a good, rich colour, select closed shaggy ink caps that have not started to blacken and deteriorate.

Oriental Beef

This sumptuously rich beef melts in the mouth, and is perfectly complemented by the piquant, crunchy relish.

Serves 4

INGREDIENTS
450 g/1 lb rump steak, cut into
    thin strips
4 whole radishes, to garnish
15 ml/1 tbsp sunflower oil

FOR THE MARINADE
2 cloves garlic, crushed
60 ml/4 tbsp dark soy sauce
30 ml/2 tbsp dry sherry
10 ml/2 tsp soft dark brown sugar

FOR THE RELISH
6 radishes
10 cm/4 in piece cucumber
1 piece stem ginger

1 Place the beef in a large, non-metallic bowl. To make the marinade, mix together the garlic, soy sauce, sherry and sugar in a bowl. Pour it over the beef and leave to marinate overnight.

2 To make the relish, chop the radishes and cucumber into matchsticks and the ginger into small matchstick pieces. Mix together in a bowl.

3 Preheat the wok, then add the oil. When the oil is hot, add the meat and marinade and stir-fry for 3–4 minutes. Serve with the relish, and garnish with the radishes.

Calf's Liver with Honey

Liver is prepared in many ways all over France and this recipe is a quick and easy, slightly contemporary treatment.

Serves 4

INGREDIENTS

4 slices calf's liver (about 175 g/6 oz each and 1 cm/½ in thick)
plain flour, for dusting
25 g/1 oz/2 tbsp butter
30 ml/2 tbsp vegetable oil
30 ml/2 tbsp red wine vinegar
30–45 ml/2–3 tbsp chicken stock
15 ml/1 tbsp clear honey
salt and freshly ground black pepper
watercress sprigs, to garnish

1 Wipe the liver with damp kitchen paper, then season both sides with salt and pepper and dust lightly with flour, shaking off any excess.

2 In a frying pan, melt half the butter with the oil over a high heat.

3 Cook the liver for 1–2 minutes, until browned on one side, then turn and cook for a further 1 minute. Transfer to warm plates.

4 Stir the vinegar, stock and honey into the pan and boil, stirring constantly, for about 1 minute. Add the remaining butter, stirring until melted and smooth. Spoon over the liver and garnish with watercress.

COOK'S TIP: Mildly flavoured calf's liver is best cooked underdone.

Veal Escalopes with Lemon

A popular dish in Italian restaurants, these veal escalopes are very easy to make at home.

Serves 4

INGREDIENTS
4 veal escalopes
30–45 ml/2–3 tbsp plain flour
50 g/2 oz/4 tbsp butter
60 ml/4 tbsp olive oil
60 ml/4 tbsp Italian dry white vermouth or dry white wine
45 ml/3 tbsp lemon juice
salt and freshly ground black pepper
lemon wedges, grated rind and fresh parsley, to garnish
green beans and peperonata, to serve

1 Put each escalope between two sheets of clear film and pound until very thin. Cut the escalopes in half or quarters and coat in the flour, seasoned with salt and pepper.

2 Melt the butter with half the oil in a large, heavy frying pan until sizzling. Add as many escalopes as the pan will hold. Fry over a medium to high heat for 1–2 minutes on each side, until lightly coloured. Remove with a fish slice and keep hot. Add the remaining oil and cook the remaining escalopes in the same way.

3 Remove the pan from the heat and add the vermouth or wine and the lemon juice. Stir vigorously to mix with the pan juices, then return to the heat and return all the veal to the pan. Spoon the sauce over the veal. Shake the pan over a medium heat until all the escalopes are coated in the sauce and heated through.

4 Serve at once, garnished with lemon wedges, rind and parsley, with cooked green beans and peperonata.

Tenderloin of Pork

This easy-to-carve cut of pork has a rich prune and mushroom stuffing, and is served with an unusual, fruity onion and prune gravy.

Serves 8

INGREDIENTS
3 large pork fillets, weighing about
    1.2 kg/2½ lb in total
225 g/8 oz rindless streaky bacon
25 g/1 oz/2 tbsp butter
150 ml/¼ pint/⅔ cup red wine

FOR THE PRUNE STUFFING
25 g/1 oz/2 tbsp butter
1 onion, very finely chopped
115 g/4 oz/1½ cups mushrooms, very
    finely chopped
4 no-soak prunes, stoned
    and chopped
10 ml/2 tsp dried mixed herbs
115 g/4 oz/2 cups fresh
    white breadcrumbs
1 egg
salt and freshly ground black pepper

TO FINISH
16 no-soak prunes
150 ml/¼ pint/⅔ cup red wine
16 pickling onions
30 ml/2 tbsp plain flour
300 ml/½ pint/1¼ cups
    chicken stock

1 Preheat the oven to 180°/350°F/
Gas 4. Trim the fillets, removing
any sinew and fat. Cut each fillet
lengthways, three-quarters of the way
through, open them out and flatten.

2 For the stuffing, melt the butter
and cook the onion until tender.
Add the chopped mushrooms and
cook for 5 minutes. Transfer to a bowl
and mix in the remaining stuffing
ingredients. Spread the stuffing over
two of the fillets and sandwich
together with the third fillet.

3 Carefully stretch each rasher of
bacon by running the back of a
large knife along its length.

4 Lay the bacon overlapping across
the meat. Lay lengths of string at
2 cm/¾ in intervals over the bacon.
Cover with a piece of foil and roll the
pork over. Fold the bacon over the
meat and secure with the string. Roll
the pork back and remove the foil.

COOK'S TIP: Tenderloin is the
choice cut for using here.

5 Place in a roasting tin and spread the butter over the top. Pour in the wine and cook for 1¼ hours, basting occasionally until evenly browned. Simmer the remaining prunes in the wine until tender. Boil the pickling onions in salted water for 10 minutes, or until just tender. Drain and add to the prunes and wine.

6 Transfer the pork to a serving plate, remove the string and leave for 10–15 minutes, before slicing. Remove any fat from the roasting tin, add the flour and cook gently for 2–3 minutes. Add the stock, boil, then simmer for 5 minutes. Adjust the seasoning. Strain on to the prunes and onions, reheat and serve immediately.

Baked Ribs

Eat these ribs with your fingers.

Serves 6

INGREDIENTS
30 ml/2 tbsp vegetable oil
1 onion, cut into thin wedges
1 garlic clove, crushed
100 ml/3½ fl oz/scant ½ cup
    real maple syrup
15 ml/1 tbsp soy sauce
15 ml/1 tbsp tomato ketchup
15 ml/1 tbsp Worcestershire sauce
5 ml/1 tsp ground ginger
5 ml/1 tsp paprika
5 ml/1 tsp mustard powder
15 ml/1 tbsp red wine vinegar
5 ml/1 tsp Tabasco sauce
1 kg/2¼ lb pork spare ribs
fresh parsley, to garnish

1 Preheat the oven to 200°C/400°F/
Gas 6. Heat the oil in a saucepan,
add the onion and garlic and cook for
about 5 minutes, until soft.

2 Add the remaining ingredients except
the ribs. Bring to the boil, lower
the heat and simmer for 2 minutes.

3 Place the ribs in a roasting tin,
pour over the sauce and turn the
ribs to coat them completely. Cover
with foil and bake for 45 minutes.
Remove the foil and bake for 15
minutes more, basting occasionally. The
ribs should be sticky and tender. Serve
garnished with fresh parsley.

Jerk Pork

A Jamaican recipe full of fire.

Serves 4

INGREDIENTS
15 ml/1 tbsp groundnut oil
2 onions, finely chopped
2 fresh red chillies, seeded and finely chopped
1 garlic clove, crushed
2.5 cm/1 in piece of fresh root ginger, grated
5 ml/1 tsp dried thyme
5 ml/1 tsp ground allspice
5 ml/1 tsp hot pepper sauce
30 ml/2 tbsp rum
grated rind and juice of 1 lime
4 pork chops
salt and freshly ground black pepper
fresh thyme, small red chillies and lime
    wedges, to garnish

1 Heat the oil in a frying pan. Add the
onions and cook for 10 minutes.
Add the spices and herbs and fry for
2 minutes. Stir in the hot pepper
sauce, rum, lime rind and juice.

2 Simmer until the mixture forms a
dark paste. Season with salt and
pepper and leave to cool. Rub the
paste over the chops. Put them in a
shallow dish, cover and chill overnight.

3 Preheat the oven to 190°C/375°F/
Gas 5. Place the chops on a rack in
a roasting tin and roast for 30 minutes,
until fully cooked. Garnish and serve.

Right: Baked Ribs (top); Jerk Pork

Paprika Pork with Fennel & Caraway

Fennel always tastes very good with pork, and combined with caraway seeds adds an aromatic flavour to this Middle European dish.

Serves 4

INGREDIENTS
15 ml/1 tbsp olive oil
4 boneless pork steaks
1 large onion, thinly sliced
400 g/14 oz can chopped tomatoes
5 ml/1 tsp fennel seeds,
  lightly crushed
2.5 ml/½ tsp caraway seeds,
  lightly crushed
15 ml/1 tbsp paprika, plus extra,
  to garnish
30 ml/2 tbsp soured cream
salt and freshly ground black pepper
buttered noodles and poppy seeds, to serve

2 Add the sliced onion to the oil remaining in the pan. Cook for 10 minutes, stirring occasionally, until soft and golden. Stir in the tomatoes, crushed fennel and caraway seeds and paprika.

3 Return the pork to the pan and simmer gently for 20–30 minutes, until tender. Season with salt and pepper to taste. Lightly swirl in the soured cream and sprinkle with a little paprika to garnish. Serve with noodles, tossed in butter and sprinkled with poppy seeds.

1 Heat the oil in a large, heavy-based frying pan over a medium heat. Add the pork steaks and fry on both sides until light golden brown. Lift out the steaks and put them on a plate.

COOK'S TIP: Always buy good quality paprika and replace it regularly, as it loses its distinctive flavour very quickly.

Pork Casserole with Coriander

This lightly spiced pork stew is really delicious served simply, as it would be in Cyprus, with warm bread, a leafy salad and a few olives.

Serves 4

INGREDIENTS
675 g/1½ lb pork fillet, boneless leg or
    chump steaks
20 ml/4 tsp coriander seeds
2.5 ml/½ tsp caster sugar
45 ml/3 tbsp olive oil
2 large onions, sliced
300 ml/½ pint/1¼ cups red wine
salt and freshly ground black pepper
fresh coriander, to garnish

1 Cut the pork into small chunks, discarding any excess fat. Crush the coriander seeds with a pestle and mortar until fairly finely ground.

2 Mix the coriander seeds with the sugar and salt and pepper and rub all over the meat. Leave to marinate for up to 4 hours.

3 Preheat the oven to 160°C/325°F Gas 3. Heat 30 ml/2 tbsp of the o in a frying pan over a high heat. Brown the meat quickly, then transfer to an ovenproof dish.

4 Add the remaining oil to the pan and fry the sliced onions until beginning to colour. Stir in the wine and a little salt and pepper and bring just to the boil.

5 Pour the onion and wine mixture over the meat and cover with a lie Bake for 1 hour, or until the meat is very tender. Garnish with coriander.

COOK'S TIP: A coffee grinder can also be used to grind the coriander seeds. Alternatively, use 15 ml/1 tbsp ground coriander.

Pork with Camembert

Most cheese-producing regions of France have a tradition of recipes using their own cheese. This recipe includes local products, such as Camembert and cider, from the Normandy region.

Serves 3–4

INGREDIENTS
350–450 g/¾–1 lb pork fillet
15 g/½ oz/1 tbsp butter
45 ml/3 tbsp sparkling dry cider or dry
    white wine
120–175 ml/4–6 fl oz/½–¾ cup crème
    fraîche or whipping cream
15 ml/1 tbsp chopped fresh mixed herbs,
    such as marjoram, thyme and sage
115 g/4 oz Camembert cheese,
    rind removed, sliced
7.5 ml/1½ tsp Dijon mustard
salt and freshly ground black pepper
fresh parsley, to garnish

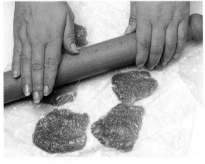

1 Slice the pork fillet crossways into small steaks about 2 cm/¾ in thick. Place between two sheets of clear film and pound with the flat side of a meat mallet or with a rolling pin to flatten to a thickness of 1 cm/½ in. Sprinkle with pepper.

2 Melt the butter in a heavy-based frying pan over a medium–high heat until it begins to brown, then add the meat. Cook for 5 minutes, turning once, or until just cooked through and the meat is springy when pressed. Transfer to a warmed dish and cover to keep warm.

3 Add the cider or white wine and bring to the boil, scraping the base of the pan. Stir in 120 ml/4 fl oz/ ½ cup of the crème fraîche or cream and the chopped herbs and gently bring back to the boil.

4 Add the Camembert cheese and mustard and any accumulated juices from the meat. Add a little more crème fraîche or cream if needed and adjust the seasoning to taste. Serve the pork with the sauce and garnish with parsley.

Thai Pork Satay with Peanut Sauce

An Indonesian dish, satay is popular all over South-east Asia.

Makes 8

INGREDIENTS

½ small onion, finely chopped
2 garlic cloves, crushed
30 ml/2 tbsp lemon juice
15 ml/1 tbsp soy sauce
5 ml/1 tsp ground coriander
2.5 ml/½ tsp ground cumin
5 ml/1 tsp ground turmeric
30 ml/2 tbsp vegetable oil
450 g/1 lb pork tenderloin, cut into
    thin strips
fresh coriander sprigs, to garnish
boiled rice, to serve

FOR THE SAUCE

50 g/2 oz creamed coconut, chopped
60 ml/4 tbsp crunchy peanut butter
15 ml/1 tbsp lemon juice
2.5 ml/½ tsp ground cumin
2.5 ml/½ tsp ground coriander
5 ml/1 tsp soft brown sugar
15 ml/1 tbsp soy sauce
1–2 dried red chillies, or ½ fresh red chilli,
    seeded and finely chopped
15 ml/1 tbsp chopped fresh coriander
    (leaves and stems)

FOR THE SALAD

½ small cucumber, peeled and diced
15 ml/1 tbsp white wine vinegar
15 ml/1 tbsp chopped fresh coriander
salt and freshly ground black pepper

1 Place the onion, garlic, lemon juice, soy sauce, ground spices and oil into a food processor or blender and process until smooth, or mix in a bowl.

2 Place the pork in a bowl, spoon over the marinade and mix well. Cover and chill for at least 2 hours.

3 Preheat the grill to the hottest setting. Thread about two or three pieces of pork on to each of 8 skewers and grill for 2–3 minutes each side, basting once with the marinade.

4 Meanwhile, make the sauce. Dissolve the creamed coconut in 150 ml/¼ pint/⅔ cup boiling water. Put the remaining ingredients into a pan and stir in the coconut liquid. Bring to the boil, stirring well, and simmer gently for 5 minutes, until the sauce has thickened.

5 To make the salad, mix together the cucumber, wine vinegar and fresh coriander. Season to taste with salt and freshly ground black pepper. Arrange the satay sticks on a platter and garnish with coriander sprigs. Serve with bowls of sauce, salad and boiled rice.

Braised Ham with Madeira Sauce

Accompanied by this rich Madeira sauce, a simple ham steak is transformed into an elegant dinner party dish.

Serves 4

INGREDIENTS
50 g/2 oz/4 tbsp unsalted butter
4 shallots, finely chopped
25 g/1 oz/¼ cup plain flour
475 ml/16 fl oz/2 cups
   beef stock
15 ml/1 tbsp tomato purée
90 ml/6 tbsp Madeira
4 ham steaks (about 175–200 g/
   6–7 oz each)
salt and freshly ground black pepper
watercress, to garnish
creamed potatoes, to serve

1 Melt half the butter in a heavy, medium-size saucepan, over a moderate heat. Add the finely chopped shallots and cook for 2–3 minutes, stirring frequently, until just softened.

2 Sprinkle over the flour and cook, stirring constantly, for 3–4 minutes until well browned, then whisk in the stock and tomato purée and season with freshly ground black pepper. Simmer over a low heat, stirring occasionally, until the sauce has thickened and reduced by about half.

3 Taste the sauce and adjust the seasoning, then stir in the Madeira and cook for 2–3 minutes. Strain, then transfer to a small serving bowl or gravy boat and keep warm.

4 Snip the edges of the ham steaks to prevent them from curling. Melt the remaining butter in a large, heavy frying pan over a medium-high heat, then add the ham steaks and cook for 4–5 minutes, turning once, until the meat feels firm to the touch.

5 Arrange the ham steaks on plates and pour a little sauce over each. Garnish with watercress and serve the steaks with the remaining sauce, accompanied by creamed potatoes.

COOK'S TIP: To make the sauce a deeper, richer colour, add a few drops of gravy browning liquid to the beef stock.

Roast Lamb with Herbs

This dish originates from southern Italy, where lamb is traditionally roasted with garlic and wild herbs at Easter.

Serves 4–6

INGREDIENTS

1.5 kg/3–3½ lb leg of lamb
45–60 ml/3–4 tbsp olive oil
4 cloves garlic, peeled and cut
   in half
2 sprigs fresh sage, or pinch of dried
   sage leaves
2 sprigs fresh rosemary, or 5 ml/1 tsp dried
   rosemary leaves
2 bay leaves
2 sprigs fresh thyme, or ½ tsp dried
   thyme leaves
175 ml/6 fl oz/¾ cup dry
   white wine
salt and freshly ground
   black pepper

3 Place the lamb in a baking tin, surrounded by the herbs. Pour on 30 ml/2 tbsp of the oil. Season. Place in the oven and roast for 35 minutes, basting occasionally.

1 Cut any excess fat from the lamb. Rub with a little of the olive oil. Using a sharp knife, make small cuts just under the skin all around the meat. Insert the garlic pieces in some of the cuts, and a few of the fresh herbs in the others. (If you are using dried herbs, sprinkle them over the surface of the meat.)

2 Place the remaining fresh herbs, if using, on the lamb, and allow it to stand in a cool place for at least 2 hours before cooking to allow the flavours to permeate the meat. Preheat the oven to 190°C/375°F/Gas 5.

4 Pour the wine over the lamb. Roast for 15 minutes more, or until the meat is cooked. Remove the lamb to heated serving dish. Tilt the pan, spooning off any fat on the surface. Strain the pan juices into a gravy boat. Slice the meat, and serve with the sauce passed separately.

Irish Stew

Simple and delicious, this is the quintessential Irish main course, usually served with cabbage for a filling supper.

Serves 4

INGREDIENTS
1.5 kg/3–3½ lb boneless lamb chops
15 ml/1 tbsp vegetable oil
3 large onions
4 large carrots
900 ml/1½ pints/3¾ cups water
4 large potatoes, cut into chunks
1 large thyme sprig
15 g/½ oz/1 tbsp butter
15 ml/1 tbsp chopped fresh parsley
salt and freshly ground black pepper
Savoy cabbage, to serve (optional)

1 Trim any fat from the lamb. Heat the oil in a flameproof casserole and brown the meat on both sides. Remove from the pan.

2 Cut the onions into quarters and thickly slice the carrots. Add to the casserole and cook for 5 minutes, until the onions are browned.

3 Return the meat to the pan with the water. Bring to the boil, reduce the heat, cover and simmer for 1 hour.

4 Add the potatoes and the thyme to the pan. Cover again and cook for a further 1 hour, until tender.

5 Leave the stew to settle for a few minutes. With a ladle remove the fat from the liquid, then pour off the liquid into a clean saucepan. Stir in the butter and the parsley. Season well and pour back into the casserole. Serve with Savoy cabbage, if liked.

COOK'S TIP: It is worthwhile doubling the quantities for this hearty stew as it freezes very well. Just remember to remove the portion of stew that is to be frozen before adding the butter and parsley to the casserole.

Shish Kebab

This is one of the most famous dishes of the Arab world. Lamb is the traditional Moroccan meat for this dish, although beef can be used.

Serves 4

INGREDIENTS
675 g/1½ lb lamb
1 onion, grated
30 ml/2 tbsp chopped fresh parsley
5 ml/1 tsp paprika
5 ml/1 tsp ground cumin
15 ml/1 tbsp olive oil
15 ml/1 tbsp lemon juice
salt and freshly ground black pepper
lemon wedges and parings to garnish
Moroccan bread, ground cumin and cayenne
    pepper, to serve

1 Trim the meat and cut it into fairly small pieces, measuring about 2 cm/ ¾ in square.

2 Mix the onion, most of the parsley, paprika, cumin, oil, lemon juice and seasoning in a bowl and add the meat. Stir, so that the meat is coated thoroughly with the mixture, and set aside for about 2 hours.

3 Prepare a barbecue or preheat the grill. Thread the meat on to metal skewers, allowing about 6–8 pieces of meat per skewer.

4 Grill or barbecue the meat for 6–8 minutes, or until it is cooked through but still moist, basting occasionally with the marinade.

5 Arrange the kebabs on a serving plate and garnish with the remaining parsley, lemon wedges and parings. Serve with Moroccan bread and dishes of cumin, cayenne pepper and salt for sprinkling over the meat.

COOK'S TIP: Moroccan cooks often intersperse lamb or beef fat with the meat, which adds flavour and keeps the meat moist. Alternatively, if using lamb, choose shoulder or fillet, where the fat is marbled through the flesh.

Meatballs in Tomato Sauce

Serve this traditional tapas dish with crusty bread and a robust red wine or as a meal for two with a bowl of pasta.

Serves 4

INGREDIENTS
225 g/8 oz minced lamb
4 spring onions, thinly sliced
2 garlic cloves, finely chopped
30 ml/2 tbsp freshly grated
   Parmesan cheese
10 ml/2 tsp fresh thyme leaves
15 ml/1 tbsp olive oil
3 tomatoes, chopped
30 ml/2 tbsp red or dry white wine
10 ml/2 tsp chopped fresh rosemary
pinch of sugar
salt and freshly ground
   black pepper
fresh thyme, to garnish

1 Place the minced lamb in a bowl. Add the spring onions, garlic, Parmesan, thyme and seasoning. Mix thoroughly, then shape into 12 small firm balls.

2 Heat the olive oil in a large frying pan and cook the meatballs for 5 minutes, turning frequently until evenly browned.

3 Add the tomatoes, wine, rosemary and sugar, with salt and pepper to taste. Cover and cook gently for 15 minutes, until the meatballs are cooked. Serve hot, garnished with fresh thyme leaves.

Noisettes of Lamb

A generous splash of Armagnac, a strong, aromatic brandy from South-west France, brings out the best in this simple meat dish.

Serves 4

INGREDIENTS
15 ml/1 tbsp vegetable oil
25 g/1 oz/2 tbsp butter
12 noisettes of lamb
45 ml/3 tbsp Armagnac
45 ml/3 tbsp dry white wine
300 ml/½ pint/1¼ cups lamb stock
10 ml/2 tsp chopped fresh tarragon
salt and freshly ground
   black pepper
tarragon sprigs, to garnish

1 Heat the vegetable oil and half the butter in a large, heavy-based frying pan.

2 Season the noisettes of lamb with salt and pepper and fry over a high heat until cooked and browned on both sides. Remove and keep warm.

3 Remove the pan from the heat, pour off the excess oil, add the Armagnac and flambé, if liked. Add the white wine and heat until reduced by three-quarters.

4 Stir in the lamb stock and chopped tarragon. Bring to the boil and simmer for 3–4 minutes. Stir in the remaining butter and season if necessary. Serve the noisettes with the sauce and garnish with tarragon.

Moussaka

Once confined to Greece, this dish is now a favourite in homes and restaurants across the continents.

Serves 4

INGREDIENTS
15 ml/1 tbsp olive oil
225 g/8 oz/2 cups minced lamb
5 ml/1 tsp ground cumin
1 red onion, chopped
25 g/1 oz/¼ cup plain flour
175 ml/6 fl oz/¾ cup lamb stock
30 ml/2 tbsp tomato purée
15 ml/1 tbsp chopped fresh oregano
1 aubergine, sliced
salt and freshly ground black pepper
Greek salad, to serve

FOR THE SAUCE
25 g/1 oz/2 tbsp butter
25 g/1 oz/¼ cup plain flour
300 ml/½ pint/1¼ cups milk
50 g/2 oz/½ cup freshly grated
    Cheddar cheese
1 egg, beaten

1 Preheat the oven to 180°C/350°F/ Gas 4. Heat the oil in a pan and fry the lamb and cumin for 5 minutes.

2 Add the onion and fry for a further 5 minutes, stirring occasionally, until soft and translucent.

3 Add the flour and cook for 1 minute. Stir in the stock, tomato purée and fresh oregano. Bring to the boil. Reduce the heat and cook gently for 30 minutes.

4 Cover a plate with kitchen paper. Lay the sliced aubergine on top and sprinkle with salt. Set aside for 10 minutes. Rinse and pat dry.

5 For the sauce, melt the butter in a pan, add the flour and cook for 1 minute. Gradually stir in the milk and cheese, season well and bring to the boil, stirring constantly. Remove from the heat and stir in the egg.

6 Spoon the lamb into a dish, lay the aubergine on top and spoon on the sauce. Bake for 45–60 minutes. Serve with a Greek salad.

Lamb Casserole with Garlic & Broad Beans

This Spanish recipe is based on stewing lamb with a large amount of garlic and sherry – the addition of broad beans gives colour.

Serves 6

INGREDIENTS
45 ml/3 tbsp olive oil
1.5 kg/3–3½ lb fillet lamb, cut into
   5 cm/2 in cubes
1 large onion, chopped
6 large garlic cloves, unpeeled
1 bay leaf
5 ml/1 tsp paprika
120 ml/4 fl oz/½ cup dry sherry
115 g/4 oz shelled broad beans, fresh
   or frozen and defrosted
30 ml/2 tbsp chopped fresh parsley
salt and freshly ground black pepper

1 Heat 30 ml/2 tbsp of the oil in a frying pan. Add half the meat and fry over a medium heat, turning the meat until it is sealed and well browned on all sides. Transfer to a plate. Brown the rest of the meat in the same way and remove from the frying pan.

2 Heat the remaining oil in the pan, add the onion and cook for about 5 minutes until soft. Transfer to a large saucepan or flameproof casserole and add the meat.

3 Add the garlic cloves, bay leaf, paprika and sherry. Season with salt and pepper. Bring to the boil, then cover and simmer very gently for 1½–2 hours, until the meat is tender.

4 Add the broad beans 10 minutes before the end of the cooking time. Stir in the parsley and serve.

Lamb Korma

This is a creamy, aromatic dish with no "hot" taste. It comes from the kitchens of the Nizam of Hyderabad.

Serves 4–6

INGREDIENTS

15 ml/1 tbsp white sesame seeds
15 ml/1 tbsp white poppy seeds
50 g/2 oz/⅓ cup almonds, blanched
2 fresh green chillies, seeded
6 cloves garlic, sliced
5 cm/2 in piece of fresh root ginger, sliced
1 onion, finely chopped
45 ml/3 tbsp ghee or vegetable oil
6 green cardamom pods
5 cm/2 in piece cinnamon stick
4 cloves
900 g/2 lb lean lamb, cubed
5 ml/1 tsp cumin powder
5 ml/1 tsp coriander powder
300 ml/½ pint/1¼ cups double cream mixed
   with 2.5 ml/½ tsp cornflour
salt
roasted sesame seeds, to garnish

1 Heat a frying pan and dry fry the first 7 ingredients. Cool the mixture and grind to a fine paste using a pestle and mortar or food processor.

2 Gently heat the ghee or oil in a frying pan. Add the cardamom pods, cinnamon stick and cloves. Quickly stir once and allow the spices to sizzle until the cloves swell.

3 Add the lamb, cumin and coriander and the prepared paste and season to taste with salt. Cover and cook until the lamb is almost tender.

COOK'S TIP: Frying spices brings out their flavour. Keep a sharp eye on them, as they can burn very quickly and easily. Remove them from the heat as soon as they start to give off their aroma.

4 Remove from the heat, cool a little and gradually fold in the cream and cornflour mixture, reserving 5 ml/ 1 tsp to garnish. To serve, gently reheat the lamb, uncovered. Serve hot, garnished with the roasted sesame seeds and the remaining cream.

Traditional Roast Chicken

Serve in the traditional way with bacon rolls, chipolata sausages, gravy and stuffing balls or bread sauce.

Serves 4

INGREDIENTS
1 x 1.75 kg/4–4½ lb chicken
4 streaky bacon rashers
25 g/1 oz/2 tbsp butter
salt and freshly ground black pepper

FOR THE PRUNE AND NUT STUFFING
25 g/1 oz/2 tbsp butter, melted
50 g/2 oz/¼ cup chopped
    stoned prunes
50 g/2 oz/½ cup chopped walnuts
50 g/2 oz/1 cup fresh breadcrumbs
1 egg, beaten
15 ml/1 tbsp chopped fresh parsley
15 ml/1 tbsp snipped fresh chives
30 ml/2 tbsp sherry or port

FOR THE GRAVY
30 ml/2 tbsp plain flour
300 ml/½ pint/1¼ cups chicken stock or
    vegetable water

1 Preheat the oven to 190°C/375°F/ Gas 5. Mix all the stuffing ingredients together in a bowl and season well.

2 Stuff the neck end of the chicken quite loosely, allowing room for the breadcrumbs to swell during cooking. Any remaining stuffing can be shaped into small balls and fried or roasted to accompany the chicken.

3 Tuck the neck skin under the bird to secure the stuffing and hold in place with the wing tips (pinions) or sew with thread or fine string.

4 Place in a roasting tin and cover with the bacon rashers. Spread with the butter, cover with foil and roast for about 1½ hours. Baste 3 or 4 times during cooking and remove the foil for the last 30 minutes.

5 Remove any trussing string and transfer to a serving plate, re-cover with the foil and leave to stand while making the gravy.

6 Carefully spoon off the fat from the juices in the roasting tin. Blend in the flour and cook gently until golden brown. Add the stock or reserved vegetable water, and bring to the boil, stirring until thickened. Adjust the seasoning, then strain into a jug or gravy boat for serving.

Chicken with Lemons & Olives

Preserved lemons and limes are frequently used in Mediterranean cookery, particularly in North Africa where their gentle flavour enhances all kinds of meat and fish dishes.

Serves 4

INGREDIENTS
2.5 ml/½ tsp ground cinnamon
2.5 ml/½ tsp ground turmeric
1.5 kg/3–3½ lb chicken
30 ml/2 tbsp olive oil
1 large onion, thinly sliced
5 cm/2 in piece fresh root ginger, grated
600 ml/1 pint/2½ cups chicken stock
2 preserved lemons or limes, or fresh, cut into wedges
75 g/3 oz/¾ cup pitted black olives
15 ml/1 tbsp clear honey
60 ml/4 tbsp chopped fresh coriander
salt and freshly ground black pepper
coriander sprigs, to garnish

1 Preheat the oven to 190°C/375°F/ Gas 5. Mix the cinnamon and turmeric in a bowl with a little salt and pepper and rub over the chicken.

2 Heat the oil in a large, heavy-based sauté or shallow frying pan and fry the whole chicken, on a moderate heat, on all sides until it turns golden brown. Carefully transfer the chicken to a deep ovenproof dish.

3 Add the sliced onion to the pan and fry gently for 5 minutes until translucent and soft. Stir in the grated ginger and the chicken stock and bring just to the boil. Pour the stock mixture over the chicken, cover and bake in the oven for 30 minutes.

4 Remove the chicken from the oven and add the preserved or fresh lemons or limes, pitted black olives and honey. Bake, uncovered, in the centre of the oven, for a further 45 minutes, until the chicken is tender and well browned.

5 Stir in the chopped, fresh
coriander and season to taste with
salt and freshly ground black pepper.
Garnish with coriander sprigs and
serve immediately.

COOK'S TIP: Preserved lemons
or limes are available in jars from
Middle Eastern stores or good
delicatessens and supermarkets.

Spicy Fried Chicken

This crispy chicken is superb hot or cold. Served with a salad or vegetables, it makes a delicious lunch and is ideal for picnics too.

Serves 4–6

INGREDIENTS
4 chicken drumsticks
4 chicken thighs
10 ml/2 tsp curry powder
2.5 ml/½ tsp garlic granules
2.5 ml/½ tsp freshly ground
    black pepper
2.5 ml/½ tsp paprika
about 300 ml/½ pint/1¼
    cups milk
groundnut oil, for deep frying
50 g/2 oz/½ cup plain flour
salt
salad leaves, to serve

2 Preheat the oven to 180°C/350°F/ Gas 4. Pour enough milk into the bowl to cover the chicken and leave to stand for a further 15 minutes.

3 Heat the oil in a large saucepan or deep-fat fryer and tip the flour on to a plate. Shake off any excess milk, dip each piece of chicken in flour and fry two or three pieces at a time until golden, but not cooked.

1 Place the chicken pieces in a large bowl and sprinkle with the curry powder, garlic granules, freshly ground black pepper, paprika and salt. Rub the spices well into the chicken, then cover and leave to marinate in a cool place for at least 2 hours, or overnight in the fridge.

4 Remove with a slotted spoon. Place on a baking tray, and bake for 30 minutes. Serve with salad.

Coq au Vin

There are many variations to this traditional French dish, but this one is especially delicious. Serve it with warm French bread.

Serves 4

INGREDIENTS
30 ml/2 tbsp olive oil
25 g/1 oz/2 tbsp butter
1 x 1.75 kg/4–4½ lb chicken, cut into
    8 pieces
115 g/4 oz gammon, cut into 5 mm/
    ¼ in strips
115 g/4 oz/1½ cups button onions, peeled
115 g/4 oz/1½ cups button mushrooms
2 garlic cloves, crushed
30 ml/2 tbsp brandy
250 ml/8 fl oz/1 cup red wine
300 ml/½ pint/1¼ cups chicken stock
1 bouquet garni
25 g/1 oz/2 tbsp butter, blended with 30 ml/
    2 tbsp flour
salt and freshly ground black pepper
chopped parsley, to garnish

2 Add the gammon strips, peeled onions, mushrooms and garlic and stir thoroughly to mix.

3 Pour over the brandy and set it alight. Pour over the red wine, stock, bouquet garni and seasoning. Cover and cook slowly for about 1 hour, either on top of the cooker or in the preheated oven.

1 Preheat the oven to 160°C/325°F/ Gas 3, if using (see step 3). Heat the oil and butter in a large flameproof casserole and brown the chicken pieces on both sides.

4 Remove the chicken and keep warm. Thicken the sauce with the butter mixture and season. Cook for several minutes and replace the chicken. Serve garnished with parsley

Roast Duck with Orange

Most of the meat is on the breast. It is easier to cut the whole breast off each side and slice it on a board.

Serves 8

INGREDIENTS
4 oranges, segmented, with rind and
　juice reserved
2 x 2.25 kg/5 lb oven-ready
　ducks
salt and freshly ground black pepper

FOR THE SAUCE
30 ml/2 tbsp flour
300 ml/½ pint/1¼ cups chicken stock
150 ml/¼ pint/⅔ cup port or red wine
15 ml/1 tbsp redcurrant jelly

1 Preheat the oven to 180°C/350°F/
Gas 4. Tie the orange rind with string and place it inside the cavities of the ducks.

2 Place the ducks on racks in roasting tins, season and cook for 30 minutes per 450 g/1 lb (about 2½ hours), until the flesh is tender and the juices run clear.

3 Halfway through the cooking time pour off the fat into a bowl. At the end of the cooking time transfer the ducks to a carving board, remove and reserve the rind from the cavities.

4 To make the sauce, remove any fat from the tin. Sprinkle in the flour and cook gently for 2 minutes. Blend in the remaining ingredients and reserved orange rind, roughly chopped. Bring to the boil and simmer for 10 minutes. Strain into a pan and add the orange segments with their juice.

5 To carve the ducks, remove the legs and wings, cutting through the joints. Cut the two end joints off the wings and discard them. Cut the breast meat off the carcass in one piece and slice it thinly. Arrange on a warm serving plate, spoon over some of the hot sauce and serve the rest separately in a sauce boat.

Braised Pheasant with Ceps, Chestnuts & Bacon

Pheasant at the end of their season are not suitable for roasting, so slow cooking is ideal. Consider this delicious casserole enriched with wild mushrooms and chestnuts.

Serves 4

INGREDIENTS
2 mature pheasants
50 g/2 oz/4 tbsp butter
75 ml/5 tbsp brandy
12 button or pickling onions, peeled
1 celery stick, chopped
50 g/2 oz unsmoked rindless bacon,
    cut into strips
45 ml/3 tbsp plain flour
550 ml/18 fl oz/2¼ cups chicken
    stock, boiling
175 g/6 oz peeled chestnuts (canned,
    vacuum-packed or fresh)
350 g/12 oz/5 cups fresh ceps or bay boletus,
    trimmed and sliced, or 15 g/½ oz/
    ¼ cup dried, soaked in warm water
    for 20 minutes
15 ml/1 tbsp lemon juice
salt and freshly ground
    black pepper
watercress sprigs, to garnish

1 Preheat the oven to 160°C/325°F/ Gas 3. Season the pheasants with salt and pepper. Melt half the butter in a large flameproof casserole over a moderate heat and brown the pheasants on all sides. Transfer to a shallow dish and pour off the remaining cooking fat.

2 Return the casserole to the heat and brown the sediment. Carefully pour in the brandy (the sudden flame will die down quickly). Stir to loosen the sediment with a flat wooden spoon and then pour the juices over the pheasants.

3 Wipe the casserole and melt the remaining butter. Lightly brown the onions, celery and bacon. Stir in the flour. Remove from the heat.

Stir in the stock gradually so that it is completely absorbed by the [flo]ur. Add the chestnuts, mushrooms, [th]e pheasants and their juices. Bring [ba]ck to a gentle simmer, cover and [co]ok in the oven for 1½ hours.

5 Transfer the pheasants and vegetables to a serving plate. Bring the sauce back to the boil, add the lemon juice and season to taste. Pour the sauce into a jug and garnish the birds with watercress sprigs.

Index

First published in 1999 by Lorenz Books © Anness Publishing Limited 1999

Lorenz Books is an imprint of Anness Publishing Limited, Hermes House, 88–89 Blackfriars Road, London SE1 8HA

This edition distributed in Canada by Raincoast Books, 8680 Cambie Street, Vancouver, British Columbia, V6P 6M9

ISBN 0 7548 0152 7

A CIP catalogue record for this book is available from the British Library

Publisher: Joanna Lorenz
Editor: Valerie Ferguson
Series Designer: Bobbie Colgate Stone
Designer: Andrew Heath
Production Controller: Joanna King

Recipes contributed by: Angela Boggiano, Carla Capalbo, Carole Clements, Matthew Drennan, Joanna Farrow, Rafi Fernandez, Silvano Franco, Sarah Gates, Rosamund Grant, Rebekah Hassan, Lesley Mackley, Norma MacMillan, Sue Maggs, Norma Miller, Jenny Stacey, Liz Trigg, Hilaire Walden, Steven Wheeler, Elizabeth Wolf-Cohen, Jeni Wright

Photography by: William Adams-Lingwood, Karl Adamson, Edward Allwright, Steve Baxter, James Duncan, Michelle Garrett, Amanda Heywood, Janine Hosegood, David Jordan, Patrick McLeavey, Thomas Odulate

1 3 5 7 9 10 8 6 4 2

Notes:

For all recipes, quantities are given in both metric and imperial measures and, where appropriate, measures are also given in standard cups and spoons. Follow one set, but not a mixture, because they are not interchangeable.

Standard spoon and cup measures are level.

1 tsp = 5 ml   1 tbsp =15 ml

1 cup = 250 ml/8 fl oz

Australian standard tablespoons are 20 ml. Australian readers should use 3 tsp in place of 1 tbsp for measuring small quantities of gelatine, cornflour, salt, etc.

Medium eggs are used unless otherwise stated.

Printed in Singapore